Homemade Lotion
41 All Natural Simple & Easy To Make Body Lotions, Body Butters & Lotion Bars

All contents copyrighted © 2014 of Lorraine White. All rights reserved worldwide. No part of this publication may be reproduced in any form or by any means, including scanning, photocopying, or otherwise without prior written permission of the copyright holder.

In no event shall the author be liable for any direct, indirect, incidental, punitive or consequential damages of any kind whatsoever with respect to the service, the materials and the products contained within. This book is not a substitute for professional medical or skin care advice.

Table of Contents

	Page
Introduction	1
Our Products are full of harmful chemicals	2
Making Your Own Natural Lotions At Home	4
Basic Set Up & Equipment Needed	5
Infusing Oils	6
Homemade Lotion Recipes	7
Velvety Vanilla Body Lotion	8
Lovely Lavender Lotion	10
Calming Rose Lotion	12
Luscious Lavender Body Lotion	13
Super Simple Sunscreen Baby Lotion	14
Sleepy Night Time Body Lotion	15
Easy Aloe Lotion	17
Anti-Aging Lotion	18
Muscle Relieving Body Lotion	20
Basic Olive Oil Lotion	22
Night Time Blend Body Lotion	23
Stress Relieving Body Lotion	25
Jojoba Moisturizing Lotion	26
Basic Organic Lotion	27
Homemade Body Butters	28
Whipped Coconut Oil Body Butter	29
Creamy Cocoa Body Butter	30
Eczema Oaty Body Butter	31
Whipped Shea Butter	32
Stretch Marks Body Butter	33
Mint Infused Body Butter	34
Youthful Glow Body Butter	36
Easy Dry Skin Body Butter	37
Cellulite Fighting Body Butter	38

Pumpkin Body Butter	40
Varicose Veins Body Butter	42
Mango & Mint Body Butter	44
Plum & Coconut Body Butter	45
Spice is Nice Body Butter	47
Cranberry Body Butter	49
Citrus Body Butter	50
Choco Mint Body Butter	51
Perfect Peppermint Body Butter	53
Homemade Lotion Bars	**55**
Dry Skin Lotion Bars	56
Three Butter Combo Lotion Bars	58
Organic Honey & Orange Lotion Bars	60
Spicy Pumpkin Lotion Bars	62
Lavender Lotion Bars	64
Calming Lotion Bars	66
Grapefruit Lotion Bars	68
Coconut Lotion Bars	70
Peppermint Lotion Bars	72
Conclusion	**74**
My Other Homemade Beauty Product Books	74

Introduction

Hello and welcome,

My name is Lorraine White and I am a wife and mother to three wonderful children. I am like most moms who have to juggle work and home life. About five years ago I started to make my own natural beauty products after I learned about some of the damaging and toxic chemicals that some manufacturers put in the products that we buy in the store.

In this book, I am giving you **41** of my **Homemade Body Lotions, Body Butters & Lotion Bar recipes.**

What makes all these recipes fabulous is how quickly you can put these together. Once you have bought a few basic ingredients then you will be able to make lots of products not only for you and your family, but for friends and colleagues too.

There is nothing better than going **NATURAL**. When you make your own lotions, body butters and lotion bars, you know **EXACTLY** what is in them and you can alter any recipe to treat particular dry and itchy skin conditions, like eczema, dermatitis or psoriasis.

You can also create natural and wholesome beauty products for treating cellulite, for adding a youthful glow to your complexion, for helping to relieve feelings of stress and anxiety, to reverse the signs of aging as well as products that are suitable for aiding relaxation and sleep.

The sky is the limit when it comes to making your own natural beauty products. You are only limited by your own imagination. Anything is possible. Are you ready to enhance your natural beauty?

Lorraine xx

Our Beauty Products Are Full of Harmful Chemicals!

It was five years ago almost to the day that I decided to **STOP** putting harsh chemicals on my skin. This was after I researched the harmful, toxic chemicals beauty product manufacturers put in our products.

They do this as a money saving exercise mainly and seem to show little if any concern for the end consumer. This makes me angry!

The more I looked into the situation, the more I found out about how these toxins silently seep into your system through your skin. I knew that day that I had to be more careful about what I put on my skin. If you have children like me, you will be concerned about what you are putting on them too.

Some of the nasty 'hidden' ingredients in some of my lotions and creams were:

- Synthetic (un-natural) fragrances
- Methlyparaben
- Oxybenzone
- Stearalkonium Chloride
- Diethanolamine
- Propylene Glycol
- Artificial colors

This is just a few that I can remember. When you look these ingredients up, like me, you will be horrified and surprised that these manufacturers get away with it. They not only get away with it, they actually make millions of dollars selling us all potentially harmful and poisonous products.

These manufacturers are so big and powerful that any attempt to try and highlight them for what they are doing generally has no effect.

Rather than accept my toxic fate, I decided to take my own health and beauty matters into my own hands and create my own products. I am proud to say that I haven't bought a shop bought beauty product in the last 5 years and I look and feel better than I have at any other time in my adult life. The treatments have knocked years off how I look and I have lovely, soft supple problem free skin.

Conduct your own research and come to your own conclusions. I would guess though that as soon as you start looking into the harmful products in your products yourself, like me you will abandon these shop bought toxic mixtures and start making your own products from the comfort of your home.

Take a look at the simple and easy recipes in this book and let's get started!

Making Your Own Natural Homemade Lotions At Home

There is nothing more satisfying than making your own natural products. Beautiful products you have created yourself out of wholesome natural and organic (where possible) ingredients.

If you implement the use of natural beauty products into your life, you will not only benefit from more radiant and glowing skin, you will also FEEL better because what you actually put ON your body actually works its way INTO your body.

All the health benefits associated with certain herbs, spices and essential oils will work their magic on you long after you have rubbed them into your skin.

Whether you are using one of the body lotions or rich creamy body butters, the whole process of massaging them into your skin on a daily basis will prove beneficial almost immediately.

Why do you think spas charge so much? They know the effect their secret (not really secret as I will show you) lotions and rubs have on the mind, body and spirit.

Making your own products at home is easy. By the time you have tried a few of the lotions and body butters on your skin you will be converted!

Basic Set Up & Equipment Needed

You really do not need much at all in terms of equipment. The following list really is enough to get started:

- A couple of glass or ceramic bowls (one small, one medium size)
- Spatula or spoon
- Weighing scales
- Small / medium sized pan
- Hand whisk or blender
- Mini chopper / food processor
- Molds (can use ice cube trays or any nice shaped silicone molds)
- Glass jars (make sure to sterilise them before you use them)

As I have been making my own products for five years now I also have a good amount of the following which I use in my recipes:

- Coconut Oil
- Shea Butter
- Cocoa Butter
- Sweet Olive Oil
- Beeswax
- Vitamin E Oil
- Essential Oils

I use organic when I can and when funds allow but you don't have to use organic only. You can get some very high grade oils and raw butters without an organic certification. I know, I've tried most of them out there.

Whatever grade you decide to use your beauty products will still be better than anything you can buy in the shop.

Infusing Oils

You can infuse your oils with herbs too if you prefer a stronger scented lotion or body butter. To do this you would simply half fill a jar with whatever herbs or fresh leaves you like (rosemary, lavender, dandelion etc) and fill the other half up to the top with your chosen oil (olive oil, coconut oil, Jojoba oil for example).

Allow the herbs/fresh leaves to infuse into the oil for at least 3 days. That way you will get a lovely strong aroma that will transfer easily into your product.

Homemade Lotion Recipes

The following homemade lotion recipes have a variety of health benefits: Please see individual recipes for further information.

Velvety Vanilla Body Lotion

What this lotion is good for:

All three oils used are natural skin moisturizers and the vanilla has natural sugars which serve to help retain the skins moisture. It also forms a protective barrier on the skin. If you are suffering from dryness and your skin needs a boost, this lotion will do the trick.

Ingredients:

- 1 cup cocoa butter
- 1/2 cup almond oil
- 1/2 cub Jojoba oil
- 1 vanilla pod

Directions:

1. Melt the cocoa butter and jojoba oil together on low heat until the two have melted together.
2. Allow the mixture to cool (20-30 minutes)
3. Add this mixture to a bowl
4. Put a slit in the vanilla pod and scrape the inside out
5. Add this to the bowl
6. Next add the almond oil into the bowl
7. Mix well and put it in a container that fits in your freezer
8. Allow to solidify (20-30 minutes)
9. Remove from freezer and whip it up using a food processor (whisk if you don't have one but this will

take quite a while) until you get your desired consistency.
10. Spoon the lotion into a glass jar and use when you feel like it
11. Enjoy your velvety smooth skin

Lovely Lavender Lotion

What this lotion is good for:

The use of lavender in this recipe means that it is suitable for all skin types. Lavender is one of the most common essential oils and is known to be beneficial at treating problem skin including acne and wrinkles. Use this lotion for a relief to dry and winter worn skin.

Ingredients:

- 1/2 cup olive oil
- 1/4 cup coconut oil
- 1/4 cup beeswax
- 1 teaspoon vitamin E oil
- 2 tablespoons shea butter
- 6 drops lavender essential oil

Directions:

1. Mix all the ingredients together (except the essential oils) in a glass jar
2. Half fill a saucepan with water over medium heat
3. Immerse the glass jar in the water so that you can melt the contents
4. Make sure to stir the mixture now and again
5. Allow to cool slightly and place it in a jar
6. Add the essential oil and mix well

7. Use as and when needed

Calming Rose Lotion

What this lotion is good for:

Great for relieving anxiety and the stresses of everyday life. The rose acts as a natural 'balancer', helping to put you in a more relaxed state

Ingredients:

- 3/4 cup rose water (at room temperature)
- 1/4 cup coconut oil
- 1/4 cup extra virgin olive oil
- 2 1/4 tablespoons grated beeswax
- 10 drops rose essential oil

Directions:

1. Heat some water in a small pan on low heat
2. Add beeswax and allow to melt (approx 20 minutes) stirring occasionally
3. Allow it to cool
4. Combine the coconut oil and olive oil in a bowl and combine
5. Put this mixture into a blender
6. Blend until the desired consistency is reached
7. Allow to cool for 5 minutes then add the rose essential oil
8. Store in a glass jar and use at your leisure

Luscious Lavender Body Lotion

What this lotion is good for:

In one word: Eczema. The National Eczema Association has stated how beneficial Coconut oil is in treating eczema, combined with the lavender it provides a calming, soothing and repairing benefit to the skin.

Ingredients:

- 1/3 cup coconut oil
- 2 tablespoons beeswax
- 7 drops lavender essential oil

Directions:

1. In a pan heat up some water on low to medium heat
2. Put the put the coconut oil and beeswax in a glass jar
3. Add the jar to the heated water and allow the beeswax to completely melt
4. Remove from heat and allow the mixture to cool
5. Add lavender essential oil
6. In a blender, blend the mixture until it resembles a soft lotion
7. Put it in a glass jar and use it at your leisure

Super Simple Sunscreen Baby Lotion

What this lotion is good for:

A great all over moisturizing lotion with added protection from the harmful effects of the sun.

Ingredients:

- 16 oz baby oil
- 8 oz Vaseline
- 4-6 sprays of sunscreen

Directions:

1. Put all the ingredients in a bowl
2. Mix with a whisk
3. Put it in a glass jar and use as required

Sleepy Night Time Body Lotion

What this lotion is good for:

With the skin softening properties of Jojoba and the calming properties of the chamomile and lavender, this lotion is perfect for using when you have had a bath or shower at night and you want to relax. Enjoy this one, it's lovely!

Ingredients:

- 3 oz coconut oil
- 6 oz jojoba oil
- 1 1/2 grated beeswax
- 8 oz distilled water (room temperature)
- 5 drops chamomile essential oil
- 5 drops lavender essential oil

Directions:

1. In a small pan, heat up some water on low to medium heat
2. Put the beeswax, coconut oil and jojoba oil in a glass jar
3. Place the glass jar in the water and allow it to heat through (stirring occasionally) until the beeswax has completely melted

4. Remove from the heat and place the mixture in a blender
5. Allow it to cool (approx 20 minutes)
6. Turn the blender on and slowly add the distilled water a little at a time
7. Add the essential oils towards the end
8. Blend to your desired consistency
9. Use just before bed and enjoy the best nights sleep you've had in ages

Easy Aloe Body Lotion

What this lotion is good for:

Suffering from sunburnt or sensitive skin? This lotion works wonders as it replenishes the skin cells. Aloe also has high levels of anti-oxidants properties which help to promote skin healing.

Ingredients:

- 1/2 cup aloe vera gel
- 1/2 cup almond oil

Directions:

1. Mix the Aloe Vera gel and almond oil in a bowl
2. Stir together until completely mixed
3. Place the mixture in a glass jar or bottle
4. Use this simple aloe lotion after you come out of the sun

Anti-Aging Lotion

What this lotion is good for:

It's good for keeping the wrinkles at bay. Aloe fights the signs of aging by replenishing the skin with the essential oils needed. Combined with Neroli, this lotion is great for calming the skin and bringing a sense of peace and harmony to how you feel.

Ingredients:

- 1 cup aloe vera gel
- 1/2 cup grapeseed oil
- 1/2 cup beeswax
- 1 teaspoon Vitamin E oil
- 10 drops Neroli essential oil

Directions:

1. Put the aloe vera gel and vitamin E oil in a bowl and set aside for 30 minutes to allow the two to naturally combine
2. While you are waiting, put the beeswax and grapeseed oil in a glass jar
3. In a small pan, heat up some water on medium heat
4. Add the glass jar to the heated water until the beeswax melts (stirring occasionally)
5. Put the mixture in a food processor or blender and allow to cool (approx 20-30 minutes)

6. Blend the mixture in 3 second bursts adding the aloe vera and Vitamin E oil
7. Keep blending until desired consistency is reached
8. Add the Neroli essential oil at the very end and blend one final time
9. Put your lotion in a glass jar until you are ready to use it
10. Enjoy this lovely anti-aging lotion and use it regularly to maintain good skin health

Muscle Relieving Body Lotion

What this lotion is good for:

Great for nice smooth skin. There's an added benefit to the lotion in helping to relieve tired and aching muscles (thanks to the rosemary) at the end of a long day.

Ingredients:

- 1 teaspoon aloe vera gel
- 1 teaspoon coconut oil
- 1 teaspoon beeswax
- 1 teaspoon cocoa butter
- 1 teaspoon glycerin
- 1/4 cup distilled water
- 1/4 cup jojoba oil
- 10 drops rosemary essential oil

Directions:

1. In a bowl combine the aloe vera gel, glycerin and cocoa butter
2. Put beeswax, coconut oil and jojoba oil in a glass jar
3. In a small pan, heat up some water on low to medium heat
4. Add the glass jar to the heated water and allow the beeswax to completely melt

5. Let the mixture cool for about 20 minutes
6. Combine the mixtures
7. Transfer to a blender (or use hand whisk)
8. Add the distilled water a little at a time
9. At the very end add the rosemary essential oil
10. Blend in small bursts until you reach the desired consistency

Basic Olive Oil Lotion

What this lotion is good for:

Good lotion for oily skin because it is non greasy. Olive oil also helps to improve the elasticity of your skin.

Ingredients:

- 1/4 cup olive oil
- 1/4 cup grated beeswax

Directions:

1. Heat some water in a small pan on low heat
2. Put the beeswax and olive oil in a glass jar
3. Allow it to melt (approx 20 minutes) stirring occasionally
4. Allow it to cool
5. Add the hot water
6. Put this mixture into a blender
7. Blend until the desired consistency is reached
8. Store in a glass jar and use at your leisure

Night Time Blend Body Lotion

What this lotion is good for:

Beautiful night time lotion that will put you in a relaxed state ready for sleep.

Ingredients:

- 1 teaspoon beeswax
- 2 tablespoons cocoa butter (melt in microwave for 10-15 seconds)
- 2 tablespoons olive oil
- 3 drops Vitamin E oil
- 5 drops clary sage essential oil
- 5 drops lavender essential oil

Directions:

1. Heat some water in a small pan on low heat
2. Add beeswax and cocoa butter allowing it to melt together
3. Allow it to cool
4. Add the vitamin E oil, clary sage oil, lavender oil and jojoba oil
5. Put this mixture into a blender
6. Blend until the desired consistency is reached

7. Store in a glass jar and use at night time after you take a bath or shower

Stress Relieving Body Lotion

What this lotion is good for:

Good for stress and anxiety, the oils in this recipe have the effect of having a calming influence on you because of the way it helps relax your muscles.

Ingredients:

- 1/2 oz rosehip seed oil (cold pressed)
- 1/2 oz evening primrose oil
- 1 teaspoon Calendula oil
- 3 drops lavender essential oil
- 3 drops geranium essential oil
- 3 drops chamomile essential oil
- 3 drops rosemary essential oil

Directions:

1. Put all ingredients in a bottle (with a lid) and shake vigorously
2. Store in a cool place and use when desired

Jojoba Moisturizing Lotion

What this lotion is good for:

Great lotion with anti-bacterial and anti-inflammatory properties. Good for joint ache and the Jojoba is one of the best natural skin moisturizers available.

Ingredients:

- 2 tablespoons lecithin
- 3 oz Jojoba oil
- 2 tablespoons shea butter

Directions:

1. Combine the above ingredients in a glass jar and mix well
2. Store in a cool place and use as desired

Basic Organic Lotion

What this lotion is good for:

It's a natural simple lotion using organic ingredients. If you only want the best stuff to touch your skin, this one is for you.

Ingredients:

- 1/2 cup organic olive oil
- 1/4 cup organic coconut oil
- 1/4 cup beeswax
- 2 tablespoons organic cocoa butter
- 10 drops lavender essential oil

Directions:

1. Heat some water in a small pan on low to medium heat
2. Put all ingredients (except essential oil) in a glass jar
3. Place the jar in the heated water and allow it to melt (approx 20 minutes) stirring occasionally
4. Allow it to cool
5. Add the lavender essential oil and combine
6. Store in a glass jar and use at your leisure

Homemade Body Butters

The following homemade body butter recipes have a variety of health benefits: Please see individual recipes for further information.

Whipped Coconut Oil Body Butter

What this body butter is good for:

Great for nourishing the skin and removing scars and dark spots.

Ingredients:

- 1 cup coconut oil
- 1 teaspoon Vitamin E Oil
- 10 drops lavender essential oil

Directions:

1. Put all the ingredients in a blender (or in a bowl if using hand whisk)
2. Whip the mixture up to your desired consistency
3. Put the mixture in a glass jar and use it as and when you feel like it
4. It is best to store it at room temperature

Creamy Cocoa Body Butter

What this body butter is good for:

Good for dry, itchy and irritated skin. The cocoa butter helps to soften your skin and the Jojoba provides much needed relief.

Ingredients:

- 1 cup cocoa butter
- 1/4 cup Jojoba oil

Directions:

1. Heat some water in a small pan on low to medium heat
2. Put cocoa butter and Jojoba oil in a glass jar
3. Place the jar in the heated water and allow the two to melt (approx 10 minutes) stirring occasionally
4. Allow it to cool
5. Put the mixture in a blend and whip it up until you reach your desire consistency
6. Store in a glass jar and use at your leisure

Eczema Oaty Body Butter

What this body butter is good for:

This oaty body butter is fantastic for treating eczema and extreme dry skin conditions.

Ingredients:

- 1/4 cup oats
- 1/2 cup almond oil
- 1/4 cup coconut oil
- 2 tablespoons hemp seed oil

Directions:

1. Grind the oats in a blender until it resembles fine flour and set this aside
2. In a pan, heat up some water on low to medium heat
3. Put the coconut, almond and hemp seed oils in a glass jar
4. Place the jar in the heated water and allow the ingredients to fuse together
5. Add the blended oats and mix well
6. Pour into air-tight containers and allow the body butter to get hard (overnight preferably)
7. Use the body butter as and when needed, paying particular attention to the areas worst affected by eczema

Whipped Shea Butter

What this body butter is good for:

Shea butter is a natural skin strengthening miracle ingredient which also has anti-oxidant and anti-inflammatory properties too. Use this body butter for treating conditions like eczema, dermatitis, hives, skin cuts and grazes.

Ingredients:

- 4 oz shea butter
- 2 tablespoons olive oil
- 10 drops rose essential oil

Directions:

1. Put the first two ingredients in a bowl
2. With an electric whisk, whisk on high speed until buttery consistency (about 5 minutes)
3. Add rose essential oil (or any essential oil of your choice) and whisk for another 20 seconds
4. Pour the mixture into air-tight glass jars or any container you like
5. Use this luscious body butter everyday to provide the best protection
6. It is best to store it at room temperature

Stretch Marks Body Butter

What this body butter is good for:

Mango butter is a skin regenerative butter which is good for treating rashes and stretch marks.

Ingredients:

- 1 cup shea butter
- 1/2 cup mango butter
- 1/2 cup almond oil
- 20 drops mango fragrance oil

Directions:

1. In a medium pan, half fill with water and heat up on low to medium heat
2. Put the shea butter and mango butter in a glass jar
3. Place the jar in the heated water and allow the butters to blend together (stirring occasionally) for about 5-10 minutes
4. Pour the mixture into a bowl and add the almond oil and mango fragrance oil
5. All the mixture to cool down a bit (about 15-20 minutes)
6. Use an electric mixer or hand whisk to whip the body butter up until you reach your desired consistency
7. Place the mixture in air-tight jars or containers and use this lovely mango butter as and when you need to

Mint Infused Body Butter

What this body butter is good for:

Putting you in a relaxed state. Use it at night, it's great.

Ingredients:

- 2 tablespoons shea butter
- 1 tablespoon coconut oil
- 1 tablespoon olive oil
- Small handful of dried rose petals
- Small handful of fresh mint
- 1 vitamin E capsule
- 10-15 drops peppermint essential oil

Directions:

1. Half fill a pan with some water and heat it up on low to medium heat
2. Put the shea butter and coconut oil in a glass jar
3. Place the jar in the heated water and allow the butter and oil to blend together (stirring occasionally) for about 5-10 minutes
4. Add the dried rose petals and mint and allow to infuse on low heat for 10 minutes
5. Add the olive oil and mix well

6. Pour the mixture into a bowl and allow it to cool down a bit (about 15-20 minutes)

7. Use an electric mixer or hand whisk to whip the body butter up until you reach your desired consistency

8. Place the mixture in air-tight jars or containers and use this lovely body butter as and when you need to

Youthful Glow Body Butter

What this body butter is good for:

Great for maintaining a youthful glow. The oils are all extremely good at helping with scars, marks and blemishes thus restoring your natural glow. This is a real skin enhancing body butter. Use it lavishly.

Ingredients:

- 1 cup shea butter
- 1/2 cup coconut oil
- 1/2 cup almond oil
- 8 drops Frankincense essential oil
- 8 drops lime essential oil

Directions:

1. Put the shea butter and coconut oil in a glass jar
2. Heat a pan of water on low to medium heat
3. Place the glass jar in the heated water and allow the mixture to melt completely
4. Add almond oil and essential oils
5. Using an electric mixer or whisk, whip the body butter up until you reach your desired consistency
6. Put the mixture in air-tight glass jars or containers of your choice and use this lovely Frankincense and Lime body butter often, it works great on the skin
7. It is best to store it at room temperature

Easy Dry Skin Body Butter

What this body butter is good for:

Reducing and eliminating dry skin. Use it daily.

Ingredients:

- 16 oz baby lotion
- 8 oz Vaseline
- 8 oz Vitamin E Cream
- 1 tablespoon cocoa butter

Directions:

1. Add all ingredients to a bowl and mix together until all the ingredients have bonded together and you reach your desired consistency
2. If the mixture is too solid, add a little more baby oil
3. If it is too runny, add a little more cocoa butter
4. Put the body butter in an air-tight container or glass jar and use, paying particular attention to the areas of your body more prone to dryness

Cellulite Fighting Body Butter

What this body butter is good for:

As the title suggests, this body butter works on the skin to reduce the appearance of cellulite.

Ingredients:

- 1/2 oz cocoa butter
- 1/2 oz beeswax
- 3 tablespoons almond oil
- 10 drops Juniper essential oil
- 10 drops lemon essential oil

Directions:

1. Heat some water in a small pan on low to medium heat
2. Put cocoa butter and beeswax in a glass jar
3. Place the jar in the heated water and allow the two to melt (approx 10 minutes) stirring occasionally
4. Allow it to cool
5. Add the almond oil and essential oils to the mixture
6. Put the mixture in a blend and whip it up until you reach your desire consistency
7. Store in air-tight glass jars or any container of your choice

8. Use this body butter to fight cellulite

Pumpkin Body Butter

What this body butter is good for:

Pumpkin contains many disease fighting properties. It is also a great moisturizer which will leave your skin super smooth. The anti-microbial properties of the cinnamon are nourishing for the skin too.

Ingredients:

- 1/2 cup pumpkin puree
- 1/2 cup coconut oil
- 1/4 cup almond oil
- 1/4 cup beeswax
- 1 teaspoon ground cinnamon

Directions:

1. Heat some water in a small pan on low to medium heat
2. Put coconut oil and beeswax in a glass jar
3. Place the jar in the heated water and allow the two to melt (approx 10 minutes) stirring occasionally
4. Allow it to cool
5. Add the almond oil, pumpkin puree and cinnamon to the mixture
6. Put the mixture in a blend and whip it up until you reach your desired consistency

7. Store in air-tight glass jars or any container of your choice

8. Use as and when desired

Varicose Veins Body Butter

What this body butter is good for:

This body butter has so many benefits, the shea, coconut oil and Jojoba oil are all natural skin softeners and conditioners and the essential oils help to balance the skin. The combination of oils all help with varicose veins.

Ingredients:

- 1/2 cup shea butter
- 1/4 cup coconut oil
- 1/4 cup Jojoba oil
- 1 tablespoon Vitamin E Liquid
- 8 drops ylang ylang essential oil
- 10 drops rose essential oil
- 8 drops lavender essential oil

Directions:

1. Heat some water in a small pan on low to medium heat
2. Put cocoa butter and shea butter in a glass jar
3. Place the jar in the heated water and allow the two to melt (approx 10 minutes) stirring occasionally
4. Allow it to cool
5. Add the rest of the ingredients and mix well

6. Put the mixture in a blender and whip it up until you reach your desired consistency

7. Store in air-tight glass jars or any container of your choice

Mango & Mint Body Butter

What this body butter is good for:

Mango has anti-aging properties and is also a natural moisturizer. Use this body butter to improve the general condition of your skin and give it a glowing appearance.

Ingredients:

- 1 cup coconut oil
- 1/3 cup almond oil
- 3 tablespoons almond oil
- 2 tablespoons mango perfume oil
- 8 drops mint essential oil

Directions:

1. Place the shea butter, cocoa butter and almond oil in a bowl
2. With a hand blender, whip the mixture up for 3 minutes
3. Add the mango perfume oil and essential oil
4. Blend again for another 90 seconds
5. Store in air-tight glass jars or any container of your choice

Plum & Coconut Body Butter

What this body butter is good for:

Fighting the aging process and warding off free radicals. This plum body butter helps to get rid of blemishes on the skin too.

Ingredients:

- 2 oz coconut oil
- 2 oz cocoa butter
- 1 oz plum kernel oil
- 1/2 oz beeswax
- 1 1/2 teaspoons plum Jojoba wax beads

Directions:

1. Heat some water in a small pan on low to medium heat
2. Put cocoa butter, coconut oil and beeswax in a glass jar
3. Place the jar in the heated water and allow the oils to melt (approx 10 minutes) stirring occasionally
4. Allow it to cool for about 10 minutes
5. Add the plum kernel oil and wax beads
6. Put the mixture in a blender and whip it up until you reach your desired consistency

7. Store in air-tight glass jars or any container of your choice

Spice Is Nice Body Butter

What this body butter is good for:

A beautiful soft body butter that will leave your skin supple and younger looking. The spice helps to plump out your skin, getting rid of fine lines and blotches.

Ingredients:

- 1/2 cup shea butter
- 1/2 cup coconut oil
- 1/2 cup olive oil
- 1-2 tablespoons cocoa powder
- 1 tablespoon ground nutmeg
- 2 tablespoons ground cinnamon
- 1 teaspoon Vitamin E oil
- 10 drops peppermint essential oil

Directions:

1. Heat some water in a small pan on low to medium heat
2. Put shea butter and coconut oil in a glass jar
3. Place the jar in the heated water and allow the oils to melt (approx 10 minutes) stirring occasionally
4. Allow it to cool for about 30 minutes
5. Mix the rest of the ingredients together and add it to the shea butter and coconut oil mixture

6. Put the mixture in a blender and whip it up until you reach your desired consistency

7. Store in air-tight glass jars or any container of your choice

Cranberry Body Butter

What this body butter is good for:

Skin regeneration and rejuvenation. It moisturizers the skin and helps to keep wrinkles at bay.

Ingredients:

- 1/4 cup coconut oil
- 1 tablespoon shea butter
- 1 tablespoon fresh cranberries (crushed)
- 2 drops orange essential oil

Directions:

1. Add the coconut oil and shea butter to a bowl
2. Using a hand whisk or electric mixer, whip the two together for 5 minutes
3. In another bowl, add the cranberries to the coconut oil and shea butter mixture
4. Allow it to cool for about 10 minutes
5. Add the orange essential oil
6. Whip it up again in the blender until you reach your desired consistency
7. Store in air-tight glass jars or any container of your choice

Citrus Body Butter

What this body butter is good for:

A great refreshing body butter that is suitable for everyday use. Will soften your skin with prolonged use.

Ingredients:

- 6 tablespoons coconut oil
- 1/4 cup cocoa butter
- 1 tablespoon Vitamin E Oil
- 2 drops lemon essential oil
- 2 drops lime essential oil

Directions:

1. Heat some water in a small pan on low to medium heat
2. Put the coconut oil and cocoa butter in a glass jar
3. Place the jar in the heated water and allow the oils to melt (approx 10 minutes) stirring occasionally
4. Allow it to cool and add the Vitamin E and essential oils
5. Mix together and allow it to harden naturally
6. Store in air-tight glass jars or any container of your choice

Choco Mint Body Butter

What this body butter is good for:

This cooling and refreshing body butter is super nourishing for the skin and great at removing scars and dark spots.

Ingredients:

- 1/2 cup cocoa butter
- 1/2 cup mango butter
- 1/2 cup coconut oil
- 1/2 cup Jojoba oil
- 2 teaspoons Vitamin E oil
- 10 drops peppermint essential oil

Directions:

1. Heat some water in a small pan on low to medium heat
2. Put cocoa butter and mango butter in a glass jar
3. Place the jar in the heated water and heat for about 5 minutes
4. Add the coconut oil and Vitamin E Oil
5. Allow it to cool for about 10 minutes
6. Meanwhile, add the cocoa powder to the Jojoba oil and mix well
7. Pour the cocoa and mango butters into the cocoa powder and jojoba oil.

8. Add essential oils
9. Put the mixture in a blender and whip it up until you reach your desired consistency
10. Store in air-tight glass jars or any container of your choice

Perfect Peppermint Body Butter

What this body butter is good for:

Again, this is a great butter for nourishing the skin and removing blemishes, scars and dark spots.

Ingredients:

- 1/2 cup coconut oil
- 1/2 cup cocoa butter
- 1/2 cup shea butter
- 1/2 cup sweet almond oil
- 1 teaspoon vitamin E oil
- 10 drops peppermint essential oils

Directions:

1. In a pan put the coconut oil, cocoa butter and shea butter in and heat up on low heat (ensuring it is completely melted and fused together)
2. Remove from the heat and allow to cool for approx 20 minutes
3. Add the sweet almond oil, vitamin E oil and essential oils
4. Put the mixture in a refrigerator to completely cool (about 2 hours)
5. Add the peppermint essential oil and mix together

6. Place the mixture in a blender and blend until you reach your desired consistency
7. Store in a glass bottle

Homemade Lotion Bars

The following homemade lotion bar recipes have a variety of health benefits: Please see individual recipes for further information.

Dry Skin Lotion Bars

What this lotion bar is good for:

As the name suggests this bar is perfect for dry skin. Use it as and when required to promote healing.

Ingredients:

- 4.5 oz beeswax
- 4 oz shea butter
- 4 oz coconut oil
- 10 drops chamomile essential oil

Directions:

1. Heat some water in a small pan on low to medium heat
2. Put all the ingredients (except essential oil) in a glass jar
3. Place the jar in the heated water and allow everything to melt (approx 10 minutes) stirring occasionally
4. Allow it to cool for 10 minutes then add the essential oils
5. Mix it together well
6. Transfer to a muffin tin, baking tray or any mold you like for them to set.
7. When set remove from tin and use one at a time

8. Keep the remaining ones in the fridge to preserve them

Notes:

Makes approximately 12 bars

Three Butter Combo Lotion Bars

What this lotion bar is good for:

All three oils used are natural skin moisturizers and the rose has a balancing effect on you. Carry this lotion bar around and use it when you feel your skin is a little dry.

Ingredients:

- 1 cup coconut oil
- 1/3 cup mango butter
- 1/3 cup cocoa butter
- 1/3 cup shea butter
- 1 cup beeswax
- 1 teaspoon vitamin E oil
- 10 drops rose essential oil

Directions:

1. Heat some water in a small pan on low to medium heat
2. Put all the ingredients (except essential oils) in a glass jar
3. Place the jar in the heated water and allow everything to melt (approx 10 minutes) stirring occasionally
4. Allow it to cool for about 10 minutes
5. Add the essential oils

6. Put the mixture in a blender and whip it up until you reach your desired consistency
7. Transfer to a muffin tin, baking tray or any mold you like

Notes:

Makes approximately 12 bars

Organic Honey & Orange Lotion Bars

What this lotion bar is good for:

This natural soothing bar will restore and renew your skin. The orange is effective at clearing aged and dull skin.

Ingredients:

- 1.5 tablespoons of raw honey
- 2 oz organic beeswax
- 2 oz organic shea butter
- 2 oz organic coconut oil
- 1 tablespoon organic olive oil
- 6 drops orange essential oil

Directions:

1. Heat some water in a small pan on low to medium heat
2. Put the beeswax, shea butter and coconut oil in a glass jar
3. Immerse the jar in the heated water and allow everything to melt (approx 10 minutes) stirring occasionally
4. Allow it to cool for 10 minutes then add the olive oil, honey and essential oils
5. Mix it together well

6. Transfer to a muffin tin, baking tray or any mold you like for them to set.

7. When set remove from tin and use one at a time

8. Keep the remaining ones in the fridge to preserve them

Notes:

Makes approximately 5 bars

Spicy Pumpkin Lotion Bars

What this lotion bar is good for:

Pumpkin contains many disease fighting properties. It is also a great moisturizer which will leave your skin super smooth. The anti-microbial properties of the cinnamon and nutmeg are nourishing for the skin too. Rub this lotion bar on your neck and arms, The Frankincense ensures it has a very calming effect on the system.

Ingredients:

- 1 oz beeswax
- 1 oz sweet almond oil
- 1/2 oz shea butter
- 1/z oz cocoa butter
- 1 teaspoon ground cinnamon
- 1 teaspoon ground nutmeg
- 5 drops Frankincense essential oil

Directions:

1. Heat some water in a small pan on low to medium heat
2. Put all the ingredients (except essential oil) in a glass jar
3. Immerse the jar in the heated water and allow everything to melt (approx 10 minutes) stirring occasionally

4. Allow it to cool for 10 minutes then add the essential oils

5. Mix it together well

6. Transfer to a muffin tin, baking tray or any mold you like for them to set.

7. When set remove from tin and use one at a time

8. Keep the remaining ones in the fridge to preserve them

Notes:

Makes approximately 6 bars

Lavender Lotion Bar

What this lotion bar is good for:

The use of lavender in this recipe means that it is suitable for all skin types. Lavender is one of the most common essential oils and is known to be beneficial at treating problem skin including acne and wrinkles. Use this lotion for a relief to dry and winter worn skin.

Ingredients:

- 2 oz beeswax
- 2 oz coconut oil
- 2 oz shea butter
- 10 drops lavender essential oil

Directions:

1. Heat some water in a small pan on low to medium heat
2. Put the beeswax, coconut oil and shea butter in a glass jar
3. Immerse the jar in the heated water and allow everything to melt (approx 10 minutes) stirring occasionally
4. Allow it to cool for 10 minutes then add the lavender essential oils
5. Mix it together well

6. Transfer to a muffin tin, baking tray or any mold you like for them to set.

7. When set remove from tin and use one at a time

8. Keep the remaining ones in the fridge to preserve them

Notes:

Makes approximately 6 bars

Calming Lotion Bar

What this lotion bar is good for:

Geranium is a natural relaxant. Quite frankly it is one of those essential oils that are good for all skin conditions and it's suitable for all skin types. It has tonnes of skin benefits. Use this daily for improving your skins look and feel.

Ingredients:

- 2 oz beeswax
- 2 oz coconut oil
- 2 oz shea butter
- 10 drops geranium essential oil

Directions:

1. Heat some water in a small pan on low to medium heat
2. Put the beeswax, coconut oil and shea butter in a glass jar
3. Immerse the jar in the heated water and allow everything to melt (approx 10 minutes) stirring occasionally
4. Allow it to cool for 10 minutes then add the geranium essential oils
5. Mix it together well
6. Transfer to a muffin tin, baking tray or any mold you like for them to set.

7. When set remove from tin and use one at a time

8. Keep the remaining ones in the fridge to preserve them

Notes:

Makes approximately 6 bars

Grapefruit Lotion Bars

What this lotion bar is good for:

A beautifully scented luscious bar. There are lots of benefits on the skin because of the high amounts of nutrients contained within the grapefruit. This lotion will give you better looking more radiant skin.

Ingredients:

- 3 oz beeswax
- 3 oz cocoa butter
- 2 tablespoons olive oil
- 3 oz coconut oil
- 2 teaspoons peppermint oil
- 10 drops grapefruit essential oil

Directions:

1. Heat some water in a small pan on low to medium heat
2. Put all ingredients (except essential oil) in a glass jar
3. Put the jar in the heated water
4. Allow the ingredients to melt together
5. Let the mixture cool down (10-20 minutes)
6. Add peppermint and grapefruit oils and mix together
7. Pour mixture into a muffin tin (or any mold you like)

8. Pop out of the tin and use as desired

Coconut Lotion Bars

What this lotion is good for:

Coconut oil is great for eczema and dry skin problems and the shea butter will provide a protective barrier to the skin and help to nourish it. If you have dry hands, rub this bar in your hands frequently throughout the day for relief and also to promote healing.

Ingredients:

- 1/2 cup coconut oil
- 1/2 cup shea butter
- 1/2 cup beeswax

Directions:

1. Heat some water in a small pan on low to medium heat
2. Put the beeswax, coconut oil and shea butter in a glass jar
3. Immerse the jar in the heated water and allow everything to melt (approx 10 minutes) stirring occasionally
4. Allow it to cool for 10 minutes
5. Mix it together well
6. Transfer to a muffin tin, baking tray or any mold you like for them to set.
7. When set remove from tin and use one at a time

8. Keep the remaining ones in the fridge to preserve them

Notes:

Makes 6-8 bars

Peppermint Lotion Bar

What this lotion bar is good for:

Good for any skin problems, acne, wrinkles, blemishes, you name it, the peppermint in this recipe will help to alleviate it.

Ingredients:

- 2 oz beeswax
- 2 oz coconut oil
- 2 oz shea butter
- 10 drops peppermint essential oil

Directions:

1. Heat some water in a small pan on low to medium heat
2. Put the beeswax, coconut oil and shea butter in a glass jar
3. Immerse the jar in the heated water and allow everything to melt (approx 10 minutes) stirring occasionally
4. Allow it to cool for 10 minutes then add the peppermint essential oils
5. Mix it together well
6. Transfer to a muffin tin, baking tray or any mold you like for them to set.
7. When set remove from tin and use one at a time

8. Keep the remaining ones in the fridge to preserve them

Notes:

Makes approximately 6 bars

Conclusion

Well there you have it, 41 of the best recipes for lotions, body butters and lotion bars. Now go and create some of them yourself and put your own unique recipes together as well.

Remember, you are not only putting a nice smelling rub on your skin because it looks and feels nice, you are putting it on your skin because of the enormous amount of moisturizing and health benefits associated with the particular oils and rubs.

You really owe it to your skin to treat it well. You will age better and you will feel better too. Self esteem is so closely wrapped up to how we look and feel about ourselves. What better way than to raise your esteem by looking after the first thing people see when they look at you, the skin you are in.

Lorraine Xx

My other books in this series:

Homemade Body Scrubs : 52 All Natural And Easy To Make Body Scrubs, Face Masks, Lip Balms And Body Washes

Homemade Beauty Products: Over 50 All Natural Recipes For Face Masks, Face Cleansers & Face Creams

Homemade Foot Spa: 48 All Natural Foot Soak, Foot Scrubs, Foot Creams & Heel Balm Recipes

Bathmania: How To Make Bath Bombs, Bath Salts & Bubble Baths

Made in the USA
Monee, IL
21 February 2023

28429489R00046